# CLASSIC
# StoryTellers

## HARRIET BEECHER STOWE

*Mitchell Lane*
**PUBLISHERS**

P.O. Box 196
Hockessin, Delaware 19707

# Titles in the Series

# C L A S S I C
# StoryTellers

## HARRIET BEECHER STOWE

Michèle Griskey

Copyright © 2005 by Mitchell Lane Publishers, Inc. All rights reserved. No part of this book may be reproduced without written permission from the publisher. Printed and bound in the United States of America.
Printing    1    2    3    4    5    6    7    8

Library of Congress Cataloging-in-Publication Data
Griskey, Michele.
Harriet Beecher Stowe / Michele Griskey.
        p. cm. — (Classic storytellers)
    Includes bibliographical references and index.
    ISBN 1-58415-375-X (library bound)
1. Stowe, Harriet Beecher, 1811-1896—Juvenile literature. 2. United States—History—Civil War, 1861-1865—Literature and the war—Juvenile literature. 3. Authors, American—19th century—Biography—Juvenile literature. 4. Abolitionists—United States—Biography—Juvenile literature. I. Title. II. Series.
PS2956.G75 2005
813'.3—dc22

                                                            2004024607

**ABOUT THE AUTHOR:  Michèle Griskey** is a writer living on an island in Washington's Puget Sound with her family. She has been writing since childhood, and her works have been published in a variety of publications including *American Fitness* and *A Cup of Comfort for Teachers*. Michèle is currently working on a middle grade fantasy novel.

**PHOTO CREDITS:** Cover, pp. 1, 3, 6, 10, 16 Getty Images; p. 22 Schlesinger Library on the History of Women in America; p. 24 Library of Congress; p. 29 Archival Research Catalog; p. 32 University of Texas Libraries; p. 38 Schlesinger Library on the History of Women in America

**PUBLISHER'S NOTE:** This story is based on the author's extensive research, which she believes to be accurate. Documentation of such research is contained on page 46.

The internet sites referenced herein were active as of the publication date. Due to the fleeting nature of some web sites, we cannot guarantee they will all be active when you are reading this book.

# Contents

## HARRIET BEECHER STOWE

Michèle Griskey

*For Your Information

Born into a large family in Connecticut, Harriet Beecher
Stowe grew up in a time of tremendous change in the
United States. Preachers and politicians debated the issue of
slavery, and Harriet was determined to speak her mind as
well. She was able to transform her thoughts and feelings
into a book that would help alter the course of history.

# Chapter 1

## THE CALLING

Harriet Beecher Stowe was furious. She couldn't believe what was happening. Congress had passed the Fugitive Slave Law. This legislation caused tremendous fear for African Americans living in the North. The law allowed Southern slave owners to go to the North, where African Americans were free, and take their former slaves back. It also encouraged citizens to help turn in former slaves. In addition, any African American could be accused of being an escaped slave. Many African Americans were unjustly arrested or kidnapped and sent to the South. Many left their jobs and homes and fled to Canada for safety.

Though Harriet wasn't African American herself, she felt the law was unfair. Like many others living in the Northern states, Harriet was against slavery. She read accounts of how slaves were cruelly treated. Stories of brutality and, in particular, the breaking up of families upset Harriet. She couldn't believe that slave owners would sell a husband or a wife away from the rest of a family. Even worse, some slave owners would sell children, separating them from their parents.

Harriet wanted to do something, but what? Living in the nineteenth century, she didn't have the opportunities that a woman would have today. Women were expected to stay home and take care of their houses and children. Since Harriet had six children, she was busy. Politically, she felt helpless. It was one thing to sit in a parlor and debate the issue, which she and others had done for many years. She wanted to do something bigger: She wanted to take action. Writing to her brother Henry Ward Beecher, a popular preacher and antislavery activist, Harriet explained, "I feel as if my heart would burn itself out in grief and shame that such things   are . . ." Yet it was a letter from Isabella, the wife of her brother Edward, that gave Harriet an idea. Sitting in her parlor, surrounded by her family, Harriet read from the letter: "Now Hattie, if I could use a pen as you can, I would write something that would make this whole nation feel what an accursed thing slavery is."

Harriet was suddenly inspired. Reportedly she stood up and declared, "I will write something. I will if I live."[1]

# FYInfo

## African American Abolitionists

Before emancipation in 1863, many African Americans escaped from slavery, fleeing to the free states and Canada. Some of them published or lectured about the stories of their lives.

In about 1797, Isabella Baumfree was born into slavery in New York. She gained her freedom just before the slaves in that state were emancipated. Later, after a spiritual transformation in 1843, she changed her name to Sojourner Truth. She began speaking out against slavery and for women's rights. She met other abolitionists and became well known for her direct and inspirational speaking style, and for her ability to sing well. Though Sojourner couldn't read or write, her story was written for her and published in 1850 as *The Narrative of Sojourner Truth: A Northern Slave.*

In 1851 she spoke at a women's rights convention in Akron, Ohio. At first many of the participants were shocked because she was African American, but she moved the audience with a powerful speech in which she repeated, "Ain't I a woman?" This became a rallying cry for many women in the years that followed. After the Civil War, Truth helped former slaves adjust to a life of freedom and taught them to be self-sufficient.

Josiah Henson

Another important abolitionist was Frederick Douglass, who had been born into slavery in 1817. His mother was Harriet Bailey, who was a slave, and his father was a white man. He managed to learn how to read and write and escaped slavery. He then became a powerful abolitionist and a popular lecturer. He published the story of his life in 1845.

After spending his childhood and early adult years as a slave in Maryland, Josiah Henson and his family escaped to Canada. They had a long and difficult journey, but after making it to freedom, Josiah went back to the United States and helped other slaves escape. In 1849 he published *The Life of Josiah Henson, Formerly a Slave, Now an Inhabitant of Canada.* This book was considered an inspiration for the character of Uncle Tom. Josiah established the Dawn Settlement near Dresden, Ontario, and helped other African Americans become financially independent.

Harriet's family included two prominent preachers, her father (center), Lyman Beecher and her brother Henry Ward Beecher (right). Both Lyman and Henry Ward were well known. The reinforcement of religion and the desire to make life better for others were important to the Beechers and strong influences in Harriet's life.

# Chapter 2

## THE BEECHER CLAN

Lyman Beecher, who was Harriet's father, was a Congregationalist minister. He and his wife, Roxana Foote, lived first in East Hampton, Long Island, where Lyman preached to a growing church. In 1800 their first child, Catharine, was born. After Catharine came William, Edward, Mary, and Harriet. Tragically the first Harriet died of whooping cough as an infant. Another son, George, was born before the family moved to Litchfield, Connecticut. There the second Harriet was born on June 14, 1811. After Harriet came her brothers Henry Ward and Charles. In 1816, Roxana Beecher died. Though Harriet didn't remember her mother very well, the memory she had was of an extremely gentle and caring woman.

Lyman remarried in 1817, to Harriet Porter, and more children arrived—Frederick (who lived only two years), Isabella, Thomas, and James.

## Chapter 2  THE BEECHER CLAN

Harriet grew up in a busy household, with many brothers and sisters as playmates. She was closest to Henry Ward. She was also fortunate to grow up in a house where everyone was encouraged to expand his or her mind. Lyman Beecher believed that his children should be strong in intellect and faith.

Harriet liked to go into her father's study and read. When she found a copy of *Arabian Nights,* she felt as if she had entered a magical world. Later she would also read *Don Quixote* and *Ivanhoe.* In addition to reading, there were lots of discussions among the Beecher clan. Lyman encouraged theological debate in the house because he believed in the power of the sermon. He often took the opposite side of an issue so that his children could improve their skills. Her debating talent would later help her tackle controversial issues in her writing.

Though Harriet was allowed to develop her intelligence and her sense of faith, she was not allowed to participate in some of the activities her brothers enjoyed. She tried very hard to do things with them when she could, but some activities, like wood chopping and fishing, were considered unladylike.

Fortunately, Harriet had other influences that gave her strength. Starting at a young age, she was able to spend a lot of time at her mother's family home, also in Connecticut, in Nut Plains. She was very close to her grandmother and her Aunt Harriet, for whom she was named. Intelligent and hardworking, Aunt Harriet taught young Harriet skills such as knitting, and both her grandmother and aunt provided motherly love and support for the little girl.

When she was eight, Harriet began attending Litchfield Female Academy. Though she was not the most diligent student—she would rather focus on only what interested her—Harriet soon found that she enjoyed writing essays. One of her essays was selected and read at the academy's annual exhibition, and her father was very proud of her.

In 1823, Catharine Beecher received awful news. Her fiancé had drowned at sea. Catharine decided to start a school for girls. At a time when women were taught more social than intellectual skills, her Hartford Female Seminary offered academic classes such as grammar, logic, and language. Catharine felt it was important that females receive the same academic opportunities that males did. Harriet enrolled in the Hartford Female Seminary when she was thirteen.

As a student, Harriet was intelligent, but also absentminded and moody. She developed a great fear that she would die young, maybe because her mother had. She was at a stage in her life where she wanted to define what she was going to do and what kind of person she wanted to become. Despite her struggles, she did well in school. In addition to studying traditional subjects, Harriet had the opportunity to edit the *Gazette,* the school newspaper.

Growing up with a minister father who had a strong desire to promote Christianity, Harriet too found a need to share her views on faith with others. This style of preaching morality and a just life was one that she used in her writing as well. In personal letters to her family and friends, and later, in her essays and stories, she would express the need for all to lead a righteous life.

13

But Harriet wasn't always serious. She also had a sense of humor and enjoyed playing jokes. Once, she and her brother Henry Ward traded clothes and dressed up as each other.

When Harriet graduated from Hartford Female Seminary, she, like most educated women during the nineteenth century, became a teacher. Other jobs were not available to women at that time. She was just sixteen years old. Her great skill was teaching what she knew best— rhetoric and composition. Harriet continued to teach with her sister Catharine until her family moved to Cincinnati, Ohio, in 1832. There, Lyman Beecher became president of the Lane Theological Seminary.

It was in Cincinnati that Harriet, with Catharine's help, wrote her first book, *Primary Geography for Children*. It sold very well. Harriet's ability to draw her readers into her discussion was a strength that she would continue to use with later literary works. She would paint a picture for her readers to imagine along with her. Soon afterward she began teaching at Catharine's new school, the Western Female Institute. Depressed, Harriet was no longer sure what she wanted to be—a writer or a teacher. What she needed was some encouragement.

# FYInfo

## Nineteenth Century Women

During the 1800s, life for women was very different than it is now. Girls were raised differently than boys. Boys were expected to get an education, find work, and provide for their families. Girls were not encouraged to be as educated as boys, because they were expected to marry, have children, and run a household. Women were to set an example of morality, cheerfulness, and obedience. Though some farm women worked outside, most women were expected to tend only to indoor duties. Unmarried women were not encouraged to work except as teachers or in textile mills. As soon as a woman was married, she was expected to give up her job.

Women were not allowed to vote, own property, or voice their opinions in public. Sometimes groups of women would go out to teach others how to be moral and worthy people like themselves. Over time, some of these groups turned toward social or political issues, such as the abolitionist movement. Abolitionism made a lot of women stop and think about their own lack of rights. Some of them felt they were treated not much better than slaves. In 1848 a group of dissatisfied women gathered in Seneca Falls, New York, to declare the need for women's rights. These suffragists, as they were called, endured a long battle to gain the vote for women. Finally, in 1920, that right was granted.

In the nineteenth century, women wore only dresses, which were long and

Elizabeth Cady Stanton

held out with wide hoops. Underneath the dresses were petticoats and corsets. A corset had whalebone and later steel sewn inside to make it stiff. In the back was a series of laces that were tied snug. The corset gave women an hourglass figure. The ideal waist size for women in the nineteenth century was eighteen inches! Many women squeezed themselves into their corsets to fit this unhealthy ideal. The corsets pressed so tightly against the body, they impaired breathing and digestion. Many doctors and clergymen warned women not to wear them, but fashion dictated a tiny waist and wide full skirts.

Some women's rights activists, such as Elizabeth Cady Stanton, decided to try an alternative to the uncomfortable dresses and corsets. Stanton wore a bloomer outfit with loose pants. These outfits were severely criticized by the general public. It wouldn't be until the twentieth century that women would gain the freedom to vote, work, own property, and wear what they wanted.

*Calvin Ellis Stowe (shown here) married Harriet after the tragic death of his first wife, Eliza. As a scholar of biblical literature, Calvin supported Harriet's writing career though he criticized her housekeeping abilities and her excessive spending habits. Calvin and Harriet were married for fifty years until Calvin's death in 1886.*

# Chapter 3

## DOMESTIC ACTIVITIES

Before television and telephones, writing was the way in which people communicated over long distances. Letters, articles in newspapers and journals, and books provided information and entertainment. Many educated people had the opportunity to write their views. Also, many literary groups formed. In these groups, writers could get together and share their work. Not long after the publication of their geography book, Harriet and Catharine were invited to join the Semi-Colon Club.

The Semi-Colon Club was a gathering of writers who met once a week for reading, discussion, and dancing. There Harriet found an interested audience for her work and a social connection with other writers and thinkers. She worked diligently there to improve her writing. In her stories, she used the conversational style that she had developed in her letter writing. Her stories were very popular. Someone encouraged her to enter a literary contest, and Harriet won $50 for her story "A New England Sketch." It was a story about "Uncle Lot," who was based on the man who raised her father.

A professor of biblical literature at Lane Seminary—Calvin Stowe—also attended the Semi-Colon Club. Harriet became friends with his wife, Eliza. When Eliza suddenly died of cholera, Harriet consoled Calvin. Eight months later, Calvin let Harriet know that he loved her. In a letter, he wrote: "I have a sort of feeling of *inseparableness,* as though my blood somehow circulated through your veins, and if you were to be torn from me I should *bleed to death.*"[1] Harriet and Calvin were married in 1836.

Harriet described herself as a "little bit of a woman."[2] She was short, with dark curls that surrounded a serious face. She never considered herself a beauty or as having any remarkable skills, but she was determined to make a life for herself and her family.

Five months after they married, Calvin sailed to Europe to buy books for the seminary and to study Prussian school methods. Harriet had to stay home because she was expecting their first child. While Calvin was still away, in September, Harriet gave birth to twin daughters, Eliza and Harriet, or Hatty, as she was called. These were the first of many births for Harriet.

As Harriet and Calvin's family grew, they found that Calvin's small salary wasn't enough to support them. They did what they could to save, and they borrowed money as well. It didn't make Harriet happy, but what could she do? She decided to do what she loved best—she would write for money. She also found writing an excellent way to communicate her ideas. Fortunately, Calvin Stowe encouraged her desire to write. His wasn't a common attitude at the time—women were supposed to focus primarily on keeping a house and raising children.

After the twins, Harriet bore a son, Henry Ellis, and then Frederick. These were trying times for Harriet, whose health and energies were taxed by having many young children and a household to run. It was difficult to find time to write. Calvin found Harriet's housekeeping less than perfect. His need for order didn't mix well with her more chaotic approach to domestic duties. Yet she continued writing, and in 1843, Harper Brothers published her first collection of stories, *The Mayflower; or Sketches of Scenes and Characters Among the Descendants of the Pilgrims*. That same year, though, tragedy struck: Harriet's brother George committed suicide. She missed him terribly. Her next child, Georgiana May, was born soon afterward.

After Georgiana's birth, Harriet began to experience strange symptoms: She couldn't use her hands, couldn't concentrate, and suffered from headaches and other neurological disorders. These symptoms were probably caused by calomel, a little pill that was widely prescribed for a number of illnesses. Made of mercurous chloride, calomel caused mercury poisoning; the pill probably did a lot more harm than good for the patients. To correct the ailments, Harriet went on a water cure, a kind of spa where patients were exposed to a lot of water in order to cure a variety of illnesses. Harriet had the opportunity to exercise, bathe several times a day, and recuperate.

In 1848, Samuel Charles or "Charley" was born, a very healthy baby and a joy for the newly recovered Harriet. But her joy was soon to be darkened by the blackest shadow. In the summer of 1849, a cholera epidemic hit the city of Cincinnati. It was unknown at the time that cholera was transmitted through unhygienic conditions, such as letting raw sewage contaminate drinking water.

As the cholera spread throughout the city, many people began to fear for their lives. Harriet wrote to Calvin, who was away, that 116 people had died in one day.[3] Toward the end of July, tragedy struck the Stowe household. Charley, just eighteen months old, came down with the disease. Harriet sat helpless beside him while the cholera took his life.[4]

The death of her child would sadden Harriet for years to come, but it would also give her an emotional connection to the slave women she would write about later. Just as she had a young child taken from her, she understood better how a slave woman might feel to have a child taken from her to be sold.

A year after her tragedy, Harriet and her family moved to Maine, where Calvin found a teaching job at Bowdoin College. He became very busy at this time, because he was asked back to Lane Seminary for one term and was also given a teaching position at Andover Theological Seminary.

Another son was born, whom they named Charles Edward after the Charley they had lost. Harriet continued to write short pieces and was soon to embark on her greatest literary achievement—the novel that would affect not only her life but also the lives of countless people who would see how inhumane slavery really was.

# FYInfo

## Cholera

Cholera was one of the first worldwide health epidemics. The disease could kill a person quickly. A person infected with cholera suffered from vomiting and diarrhea, and the extremities and face would turn bluish and stiff. Ultimately, victims died from dehydration. After infection, 50 percent of all adults and most young children and the elderly died of the disease. During the nineteenth century, there was no effective way to treat cholera. In 1817 an outbreak in Calcutta, India, soon spread to neighboring countries.

Cholera raced across Europe in 1831. Americans were highly fearful that the disease would cross the Atlantic and come to the United States. In 1832 their fears came true. Cholera came with European immigrants to Canada, killing over two thousand people there in one year. It soon spread south to the United States. What wasn't known at the time is that the disease is a bacteria spread through water or food contaminated by human waste.

The Industrial Revolution attracted hordes of people to factory work in cities. Since many growing cities, such as Cincinnati, did not have adequate sewage systems, the water supply was not clean. At that time, the cause of cholera was thought to be "bad air." Many people sealed their windows to keep out the night air. They thought individuals were infected when some sort of vapor was taken into the lungs.

Louis Pasteur

A doctor in London named John Snow argued against the idea that cholera was an airborne disease. The medical community initially ignored him. During an outbreak in 1854, he was able to trace the disease to various water pumps in London. This proved that the disease was spread through unclean water.

After Dr. Snow's discovery, changes were made in providing clean water and appropriate septic systems in cities, and the number of cholera outbreaks fell dramatically. Then in 1883, based on the germ theory work of Louis Pasteur, Robert Koch first identified the comma-shaped cholera bacterium under a microscope. Improving water-purifying systems helped eliminate the problem of cholera epidemics in Europe and the United States.

Cholera still occurs in areas where water or food supplies are contaminated with human waste. Fortunately, the disease is highly treatable now. Patients who are given fluids and antibiotics usually recover.

Harriet's writing was an opportunity for her to step outside of her own life as a 19<sup>th</sup> century woman. It was through her writing that she could express her ideas about slavery and other controversial issues. Writing opened Harriet's life to a world of possibilities including the end of slavery, which Harriet experienced in her lifetime.

# Chapter 4

## THE COMING TRANSFORMATION

In the early nineteenth century, a movement spread across the northern United States. Former black slaves joined forces with white women and men to create a new vision for a country without slaves. These people called themselves abolitionists, and they used a variety of means to get their message across. An evangelical movement began to discuss the immorality of slavery. In 1831, Arthur and Lewis Tappan joined forces with William Lloyd Garrison and started the abolitionist publication *The Liberator.* The movement gathered momentum, and in 1833 the men cofounded the American Anti-Slavery Society.

Early on the abolitionists faced a dangerous battle. Many of the more vocal members were attacked. In 1837, Elijah P. Lovejoy, an abolitionist editor, was murdered.

Women who felt slavery was immoral because it broke up families worked hard at getting national attention for their cause. Some women involved themselves in social activities including sewing circles and passing around petitions to send to Congress to show their opposition to slavery.

*The abolitionist William Lloyd Garrison published the Anti-Slavery paper* The Liberator *from 1831 to 1865. Garrison believed all slaves should be free. Though he was considered radical, he believed the emancipation of African Americans should be done through peaceful means.*

Unfortunately, though the petitions were sent to Congress, they were not always read. Proslavery senators imposed a gag rule on the discussion of freeing the slaves. This rule was in effect from 1836 to 1844.

Some women took more radical approaches to abolition. Angelina and Sarah Grimké, who grew up on a plantation, lectured for equality for all African Americans. Lydia Maria Child, who in 1833 wrote *An Appeal in Favor of That Class of Americans Called Africans,* also advocated that African Americans be treated as equals. Unfortunately, many people at that time, even some of the abolitionists, did not believe that equality should exist among the races.

Within the abolitionist movement there was a number of suggestions about how to eradicate the problem of slavery. Some Northerners believed that African Americans should be free but not equal to whites. Others believed that people from all races should be treated equally. Some believed that women shouldn't get involved in the movement; others disagreed. Some abolitionists used violence to make their point; others believed in using the power of words over weapons.

With all of this cultural turmoil, it was impossible for Harriet Beecher Stowe, along with many of her siblings, to ignore the abolitionist movement. As the unrest increased, Stowe found it hard to remain an observer. The same year that Lovejoy was murdered, a clash took place in Cincinnati between an abolitionist, James G. Birney, who ran an antislavery journal called the *Philanthropist,* and those who supported slavery. Those who supported Birney were members of the American Anti-Slavery Society. A mob of men who didn't like what Birney and the others stood for broke into Birney's office and destroyed his press. Then they destroyed the homes of some African American citizens.

Harriet Stowe and Henry Ward Beecher expressed their outrage in the *Cincinnati Journal*. Beecher, who was the temporary editor of the paper at the time, wrote a long, detailed editorial, and Stowe wrote a story about two men named Franklin and Mr. L., who talk about the violent events in the city. In their conversation, Franklin reminds Mr. L. that the mob that destroyed Birney's printing press was attacking his right to express his beliefs. Franklin also reminds Mr. L. that free speech is protected in the First Amendment of the Constitution. By using a story to express her ideas, Stowe was able to draw her readers into a believable situation—a dinner conversation between two men. Because it was still not acceptable for women to express their strong political views, she also signed the story as "Franklin."

In the years following the incident in Cincinnati, Henry Ward Beecher began publicly lecturing against slavery. His speeches were inspiring and exciting, and he gained a big following. Stowe continued to write short pieces against slavery as well. Some of these pieces were published in the abolitionist journal *National Era*. The editor liked Stowe's work and encouraged her to write more.

In 1850, the Fugitive Slave Law was passed. Incidents in which citizens were violently seized from their jobs and sent to jail enraged people of all races. Harriet Beecher Stowe was one of these people. She felt enormous anger toward those who mistreated the innocent. She was also impatient with the intellectual debates that dominated the slavery question.

Stowe felt that the most basic commonality between people was their emotions. Didn't African Americans experience the same emotions as white Americans? She wanted to express this and, as a woman living in those times, there was only one way she could—through her writing.

In June 1851, the first of her series of short sketches about slavery was published in the *National Era.* Stowe had no idea at that time that these short sketches would become a novel. With Calvin's busy schedule and six children to look after, Stowe received a lot of help from her servants and her sisters Catharine, who moved in to take care of the children, and Isabella, who copied the manuscript for her. Harriet wrote these sketches for eleven months, and many readers followed the story.

"My vocation is simply that of a painter, and my object will be to hold up in the most lifelike and graphic manner possible Slavery," Stowe wrote in a letter.[1]

Catharine wrote to the company that published Harriet's educational writings to see if they would publish *Uncle Tom's Cabin or Life Among the Lowly,* in book form. Phillips, Sampson, & Co. turned it down because they felt that a book, written by woman, about a controversial subject wouldn't sell well. Another publisher, John P. Jewett, published the novel in March 1852. The book sold 10,000 copies within the first week. By the end of the first year, it had sold 300,000 copies in the United States and 200,000 in England. Stowe earned $10,000 in her first three months of sales. This was a considerable amount of money for her once struggling family. More importantly, Harriet Beecher Stowe did something that others could not: She showed the human side to the slavery debate. She managed to touch people's emotions by showing slavery as a cruel practice.

Translated into dozens of languages, *Uncle Tom's Cabin* reached many other countries in Europe as well. In 1853 Harriet took her first trip to Great Britain, where the novel was very popular. Crowds of fans greeted her when she arrived in Liverpool. As she traveled, she met with antislavery groups. Likewise when she returned, she found herself in high demand as a speaker in the antislavery movement.

What made Harriet Beecher Stowe's work so popular? She herself had never lived in the South, nor had she experienced life on a plantation firsthand. But she had heard and read stories. Some of her information came from narratives written by former slaves. Frederick Douglass, Josiah Henson, and others wrote autobiographies. Stowe had heard tales of slaves being mistreated. Men had been whipped and women raped by cruel slave owners. These outrages upset Stowe, and she had been determined to expose it all in her writing.

One story that had caught her attention was that of a young woman's escape. In one of the most powerful parts of the novel, Stowe describes young Eliza escaping with her son. This was based on a real story of a woman who, when she found out that she would be sold and taken from her children, escaped with the youngest of her six children—a girl. She leaped across the frigid Ohio River, the border between the South and the North, by jumping from ice floe to ice floe. When the woman reached the other side, the Rankin family, who were part of the Underground Railroad, took her in. The woman and her daughter disguised themselves as males and escaped to Canada. Later, she returned to get the rest of her family. Stowe felt a great deal of pity for this woman and other women like her who faced being parted from their children. This emotional connection is what she wanted to share with her readers.

Born a slave, Frederick Douglass escaped slavery in 1838. Published in 1845, Narrative of the Life of Frederick Douglass *became one of the many influences for* Uncle Tom's Cabin. *Douglass was a powerful activist who traveled and spoke out for the rights of the oppressed. He also served as a Stationmaster for the Underground Railroad.*

Stowe also revealed through the novel's characters the effect that Charley's death had had on her. In a letter to Eliza Cabot Follen, a writer of children's books, she refers to the summer she lost her son: "I allude to this here because I have often felt that much that is in that book had its root in the awful scenes and bitter sorrow of that summer. It has left now, I trust, no trace on my mind except a deep compassion for the sorrowful, especially for mothers who are separated from their children."[2]

In another part of the book is a lovable slave owner's child named Evangeline, or "little Eva." She is kind to Tom and all the other slaves on the plantation. She dies at a young age, and Stowe was probably remembering the death of her own Charley when she wrote about her. Many other parents reading the passage probably identified as well. In a time before clean water supplies and vaccinations, diseases took the lives of many more children than they do now.

After the publication of *Uncle Tom's Cabin,* Eva became one of the most popular names for baby girls. Naming children after characters wasn't the only change brought about by the book. Soon there were songs and plays based on the novel, and pictures, mugs, lamps, and even handkerchiefs depicting scenes from the story. In fact, for almost 100 years after the publication of the novel, advertisers used the characters to sell a variety of products, from tobacco to root beer.[3]

# FYInfo

## The Underground Railroad

Harriet Tubman

In the dark of the night a group of people gathered in the woods. Bringing only what they could carry, they met a conductor, a person who would lead them through the dark woods or swamps to stations, places where the travelers could find food, a warm place to sleep, and encouragement. Some of the travelers went to ports and were smuggled onto boats. The journey was long and dangerous. If they were caught, they faced beatings or even death.

These were the passengers on the Underground Railroad, people who escaped slavery in the South to find freedom. But the Underground Railroad was not really a railroad at all. It was a system developed at the end of the eighteenth century. A group of people of all races living in the North took great chances by harboring runaway slaves in their houses. These people hid, fed, and sometimes even gave the refugees money as they made their difficult journey to freedom. Some slaves also headed south to Mexico or the Caribbean.

As the escape system developed, it was dubbed the Underground Railroad. Sometimes the stations of the railroad were the homes of people who belonged to religious groups that opposed slavery, such as the Quakers and the Methodists. Many other abolitionists also joined in assisting runaway slaves to freedom.

One of the best-known conductors was Harriet Tubman, a former slave who escaped in 1849. She made nineteen trips back to Maryland to help other people escape. It is estimated that she helped 300 people to freedom. Harriet Tubman was called the "Moses of her people," because, like the biblical Moses, she helped her people escape slavery. She worked hard keeping up the morale of the people she helped. Some of her techniques were a bit harsh by today's standards. For example, if someone lost faith and wanted to return, she would pull out a gun and threaten to kill the reluctant passenger. Nevertheless, her amazing courage in returning again and again to where she could be captured or killed reveals her dedication to help others.

Another person who helped in the Underground Railroad was Levi Coffin. Levi and his wife were Quakers. In Newport, Indiana, and in Cincinnati, his house was one of the main stations on the railroad. He helped over 3,000 people escape to the North and Canada.

After the publication of Uncle Tom's Cabin, Harriet continued to write and had the opportunity to travel to Europe where many wanted to meet her. The rest of her life was full of both the pleasures of enjoying her newfound fame and wealth and the pain of losing family members.

# Chapter 5

## THE WRITER
## AND THE WAR

As *Uncle Tom's Cabin* grew in popularity, some critics, especially those from the South, responded harshly. They questioned the origins of Stowe's material and accused her of lying about the conditions of slaves. Some even considered her unladylike for writing such a novel, one that showed slavery as a cruel institution. Stowe was surprised and indignant that the validity of her story was being challenged. Though her work was fiction, she had based it on true stories. She published *A Key to Uncle Tom's Cabin* soon afterward. The book showed how all the characters and events in the story were based on real events and real people.

An 1852 review of *Uncle Tom's Cabin* published in *The Southern Literary Messenger* shows how some Southerners felt Stowe's portrayal of slavery was not based on fact:

"We have said that Uncle Tom's Cabin is a fiction. It is a fiction throughout; a fiction in form; a fiction in its facts; a fiction in its representations and coloring; a fiction in its statements; a fiction in its sentiments; a fiction in its morals; a fiction in its religion; a fiction in its inferences; a fiction equally with regard to the subjects it is designed to expound, and with respect to the manner of their exposition. It is a fiction, not for the sake of more effectually communicating truth; but for the purpose of more effectually disseminating a slander."[1]

Many Southerners who accused Stowe argued that in reality, slaves were content. They promoted the image of the happy slave living a carefree life under the protection of a kind master. When *Uncle Tom's Cabin* became even more popular, parodies of the novel appeared, but instead of revealing the horrors of slavery, these novels showed slaves enjoying their lives in the South. A number of "Anti-Tom" novels were published, such as John W. Page's *Uncle Robin, in His Cabin in Virginia, and Tom Without One in Boston*. Many who supported slavery tried to convince slaves and others that life in the North was harsh and unpredictable. There was no guarantee that an escaped slave could find a job or a place to live. Instead slaves would be taken care of in the South.

Despite the warnings, the prospect of freedom, even with risks, was too powerful a force for many living in slavery. The impact of *Uncle Tom's Cabin* continued to grow. The story of Uncle Tom was even taken to the stage. Some of the stage productions accurately portrayed Stowe's intentions. Unfortunately, some people decided to "reinterpret" the story to reflect proslavery views. The pious and kind character of Uncle Tom in Stowe's book was turned into a bumbling stereotype of a slave unable to think for himself and who is in total obedience to his slave owner. In fact, these dramatic misrepresentations of Uncle Tom are probably where the derogatory term *Uncle Tom* originated.

In the years following the publication of *Uncle Tom's Cabin,* Stowe's newfound fame made her popular with many abolitionists. With her money and influence, she set about helping others. She felt it was her duty to help those who didn't have a way to communicate their stories to the world.

Stowe enjoyed her wealth. She traveled extensively and bought things that she had had to live without before. Calvin Stowe warned her that her spending habits were excessive, and he was probably right. Yet her love of nice things kept Harriet busy as a writer. The more she wrote, the more money she could make. In 1853, the Stowe family moved to Andover, Massachusetts. Calvin began teaching at Andover Theological Seminary. Harriet continued to write articles, and in 1854 she published a travel guide for Europe called *Sunny Memories of Foreign Lands* based on her travels.

Meanwhile, violence increased between the North and South. In 1854 the Kansas-Nebraska Act allowed two new U.S. territories to be either free or slave owning states. Protests followed. Henry Ward Beecher condemned the act. He raised money to send rifles to the settlers as protection against proslavery groups. These rifles were called "Beecher's Bibles."

Leaving the settlers in the territories to decide the slavery issue created a great deal of violence. In 1856, proslavery groups burned and destroyed property in

Lawrence, Kansas. In retaliation, a radical antislavery activist, John Brown, ordered the murder of five slave owners.

Back in the nation's capital, Senator Charles Sumner of Massachusetts gave a proslavery speech. He had some harsh words for, in particular, Senator Stephen Douglas of Illinois and Senator Andrew Pickens Butler of South Carolina. A few days later he was attacked and beaten by Butler's nephew, Representative Preston S. Brooks. The injuries were so extensive that it took Sumner three years to recover.

During these times of increasing violence, Harriet Beecher Stowe was working on her next novel, *Dred: A Tale of the Great Dismal Swamp.* In a letter, she lashed out, "How the blood and insults of Sumner and the sack of Lawrence burn within us I hope to make a voice to say."[2]

She focused this novel on a different kind of slave hero. Instead of the dutiful and well-mannered Uncle Tom, she created Dred, a more aggressive character who imagines that he is like Moses for the oppressed slaves he must liberate. Unfortunately, the novel was rushed, and consequently the story lacked proper development. It wasn't as popular as *Uncle Tom's Cabin.*

After a trip through Europe in 1857, another tragedy jolted Harriet. Her eldest son, Henry, had gone swimming with some college friends. He got caught in a strong current in the Connecticut River and drowned. Now Harriet had outlived two of her children.

Meanwhile, a real person named Dred was stirring up emotions. The Dred Scott decision by the Supreme Court was a blow to the rights of slaves and former slaves. In this decision, a slave, Dred Scott, legally sought his freedom because he had lived with his owners for seven years in "free" states. The Supreme Court concluded that Scott did not have any rights because he was a slave. Their conclusion was that slaves were not citizens of the United States.

This controversial decision caused more anger on both sides of the slavery issue. Abraham Lincoln thought the decision was horrible and began to speak out publicly against it. In 1860, he was elected president. When this happened, a number of Southern states seceded from the United States. On April 12, 1861, when a federal ship sailed in to restock supplies in Fort Sumter in Charleston, South Carolina, the Southern Rebels attacked and the Civil War began.

As soon as the war started, Harriet Beecher Stowe's son Frederick joined the Union Army. Harriet worried about her son fighting in a war. She also worried about his willpower, for since the age of sixteen, Fred had been struggling with alcoholism.

Harriet turned her energies toward writing novels on other topics. *The Pearl of Orr's Island* takes place in Maine, and *Agnes of Sorrento* was inspired after her visit to Italy.

The Civil War continued, and after some Northern successes against the South, the Emancipation Proclamation was drafted. This paper declared that all slaves would be freed as of January 1, 1863. Stowe felt tremendous hope that her great desire to see the end of slavery would soon be reality.

In November 1862 Stowe traveled to Washington, D.C., to visit Fred and the President of the United States. She was invited to tea at the White House in early December.

Legend has it that President Lincoln said the following when he met her: "So you are the little woman who wrote the book that started this great war!" Legend or not, *Uncle Tom's Cabin* did change a lot of peoples' views on slavery.

The same "little woman" was invited to Boston Music Hall on January 1, 1863, to celebrate emancipation with other

Harriet's son Frederick Stowe joined the Union Army. Fred wrestled with alcoholism and wanted to make his life better. After serving and being wounded in the battle of Gettysburg, Fred went to California in 1870 and was never heard from again.

abolitionists. At one point the crowd chanted her name, "Harriet Beecher Stowe!" They wanted her to stand so that they could acknowledge her commitment and contributions to ending slavery.[3]

After the Civil War, Stowe continued to write and travel. She bought a winter house in Florida so that she and her family could escape the New England cold every year, and where she would be more comfortable writing. She completed another novel, *Oldtown Folks,* which was published in 1869. She also began to follow the social movement for women's rights. Two important leaders of the movement, Elizabeth Cady Stanton and Susan B. Anthony, wanted Stowe to write for their publication, *Revolution.* Writing for such a publication was a little too radical for Stowe's tastes. Instead she focused her energies on the article "The True Story of Lady Byron's Life," in which she related a story that had been told to her years before when she met poet Lord Byron's wife. In the article she reveals that Lord Byron had mistreated Lady Byron.

Stowe was very nervous about publishing the article because she knew it would be controversial; however, she felt that the life of Lady Byron had been overlooked and that the public focused too much on the greatness of her husband. Specifically, Lady Bryon accused her husband of having an affair with his half sister, Augusta Leigh. Wanting to continue her tradition of speaking for the mistreated, Stowe used her power of writing to set things right. Unfortunately, it didn't.

Critics lashed out that the article didn't show anything new and that it was an inappropriate thing to write about. Unlike *Uncle Tom's Cabin,* for which Stowe could defend her point of view with proof that slaves had been mistreated, the article was based only on a conversation between Stowe and Lady Bryon, whom many believed had lost her mind. Stowe defended her work, but few others did.

Stowe then wrote *Lady Byron Vindicated* using Byron's poetry to show that she was correct. The book was also critiqued savagely. Elizabeth Cady Stanton defended Stowe, saying that many women were oppressed by their husbands, but most other critics were not impressed by Stowe's accusations. Though Stowe believed that women deserved rights, she decided to bow off center stage. She then wrote other pieces on women's rights, but she took a more conservative view, and she lashed out against the more radical women in the movement. However, her role as a major reformer of public opinion was over.

Other problems were brewing in Stowe's family life. Fred was in trouble again. Frequent treatments to cure his alcoholism didn't last. During the war he had been wounded in the horrific battle of Gettysburg. In addition, his mother's fame contrasted sharply with the failure he felt with himself. In 1870, after continued attempts to cure his alcoholism had failed, Fred went to California and disappeared. Harriet never learned what finally became of her troubled son; it remains a mystery. As with the deaths of her other sons, she mourned the disappearance of Fred.

The years that followed were both happy and sad for Harriet Beecher Stowe. She helped her daughter Georgiana with the birth of her first grandchild, Freeman Allen, in 1870. Her last remaining son, Charley, left school to become a sailor. After some time at sea, he returned and became a minister, settling in Maine. Harriet was happy to have Charley working in a profession so close to her heart. She continued to write and lecture during this time. Her final novel, *Poganuc People: Their Loves and Lives,* was published in 1878.

In 1886, after a long illness, her husband of fifty years, Calvin, died. The following year Harriet's beloved brother Henry Ward died. A few months later she also lost her daughter Georgiana, who had battled a morphine addiction for many years. In the nineteenth century it was common for doctors to give morphine for a number of ailments, including the pains of childbirth (which may have been when Georgiana had become addicted). Little was known then of the possible dangers of the drug. Georgiana was only forty-four years old when she died.

In 1889 Harriet began experiencing dementia and declined rapidly. She had trouble recognizing people she knew. She died in 1896.

With her death went a great writer and storyteller who told the tales of those who were oppressed and downtrodden. Like the lamps on houses welcoming those on the Underground Railroad, Harriet Beecher Stowe's writing illuminated the struggles of a people desperate for freedom.

# FYInfo

## Henry Ward—Harriet's Favorite Brother

Henry Ward Beecher

Like his famous sister, Henry Ward Beecher grew up under the strong influence of his father. Versed in both oral and written persuasion, Henry became one of the most influential leaders of the abolitionist movement. In 1837 he was ordained a Presbyterian minister and developed a following for his great oratorical skills. In 1847 he became the minister at Plymouth Congregational Church in Brooklyn, New York. Over 2,500 people attended his weekly sermons. There he spoke out against slavery and in favor of women's suffrage, temperance, and evolution. Unlike his father, who believed that people should live in fear of God and that sinning would produce great suffering, Henry showed more compassion for his fellow humans.

On a trip to England during the Civil War, Henry tried to persuade the English people to support the Union causes of the war. Though many of the English were against slavery, many were worried about the cotton trade from the South. Because of the war, cotton wasn't being sent to England, and many textile workers lost their jobs. Henry had a difficult time persuading hostile groups to see the value of freedom for everyone. In his signature personal style, he spoke to the people and focused on their concerns. He was very successful in altering the view of the English people during the war.

In addition to preaching, Henry wrote a number of works, including *Seven Lectures to Young Men, Life of Jesus Christ, Yale Lectures on Preaching,* and *Evolution and Religion.* He also edited the journals *Independent* and *Christian Union.*

In 1872 a shocking incident stunned those who knew Henry Ward. Writer and women's rights activist Victoria Woodhull published an article declaring that Henry had had an affair with Elizabeth Tilton, the wife of Theodore Tilton, who had been Henry's friend. Elizabeth had originally confessed to her husband in 1870 but later retracted her statement. After the scandal was made public, Theodore Tilton sued Henry, and a highly publicized trial followed. The result was a hung jury, so he was acquitted. Meanwhile, Henry's church continued to support him.

Henry died on March 8, 1887, of a cerebral hemorrhage.

# CHRONOLOGY

**1811**   Harriet Elizabeth Beecher is born June 14 in Litchfield, Connecticut

**1816**   Her mother, Roxana Beecher, dies

**1819**   Begins school at the Litchfield Academy

**1824**   Enrolls in Catharine Beecher's Hartford Female Seminary

**1827**   Graduates from Hartford Female Seminary and begins teaching there

**1832**   Beecher family moves to Cincinnati; Harriet begins teaching at Catharine's new school, the Western Female Institute; publishes her first book, *Primary Geography for Children*

**1836**   Marries Calvin Ellis Stowe

**1849**   Son Charley dies of cholera

**1850**   Moves to Brunswick, Maine

**1851**   Starts writing *Uncle Tom's Cabin,* which is published monthly in the National Era

**1852**   *Uncle Tom's Cabin* is published as a book

**1853**   Moves to Andover, Massachusetts

**1857**   Son Henry Ellis drowns

**1862**   Meets President Abraham Lincoln

**1870**   Son Frederick moves to California and disappears

**1878**   Sister Catharine dies

**1886**   Calvin Stowe dies

**1887**   Brother Henry Ward dies; daughter Georgiana dies

**1896**   Harriet Beecher Stowe dies on July 1

# SELECTED WORKS

**1832**   *Primary Geography for Children* (with Catharine Beecher)

**1843**   *The Mayflower*

**1852**   *Uncle Tom's Cabin*

**1853**   *A Key to Uncle Tom's Cabin*

**1856**   *Dred: A Tale of the Great Dismal Swamp*

**1859**   *The Minister's Wooing*

**1862**   *The Pearl of Orr's Island*

**1862**   *Agnes of Sorrento*

**1869**   *Oldtown Folks*

**1869**   *The True Story of Lady Byron's Life*

**1870**   *Lady Byron Vindicated*

**1872**   *Sam Lawson's Oldtown Fireside Stories*

**1873**   *The New Housekeeper's Manual* (with Catharine Beecher)

**1878**   *Poganuc People: Their Loves and Lives*

# TIMELINE IN HISTORY

| | |
|---|---|
| **1761** | The song "Twinkle, Twinkle Little Star" is published in France |
| **1775** | Alexander Cummings invents a flush toilet |
| **1776** | The Declaration of Independence is signed |
| **1796** | Edward Jenner invents the smallpox vaccination |
| **1800** | Count Alessandro Volta invents the battery |
| **1832** | Cholera pandemic spreads to United States |
| **1837** | Samuel Morse invents Morse Code |
| **1845–1850** | Great Famine in Ireland kills perhaps a million people and causes a wave of emigration |
| **1850** | The Fugitive Slave Law is passed |
| **1857** | The Dred Scott decision declares slaves are not U.S. citizens |
| **1859** | Charles Darwin's *Origin of Species* is published and the debate over evolution begins |
| **1861–1865** | The Civil War is fought in the United States |
| **1863** | The Emancipation Proclamation frees the slaves |
| **1865** | Congress ratifies the Thirteenth Amendment, which prohibits slavery in the United States |
| **1883** | Robert Koch identifies the cholera bacterium |
| **1900** | Count Ferdinand von Zeppelin invents the first rigid airship, called the zeppelin |
| **1914–1918** | World War I is waged |
| **1920** | The Nineteenth Amendment to the Constitution is passed, giving women the right to vote |
| **1939–1945** | World War II is waged |
| **1946** | Percy Spencer invents the microwave oven |
| **1953** | Texas Instruments invents the first transistor radio |
| **1960** | John F. Kennedy is elected as President of the United States |
| **1968** | Civil Rights Leader Martin Luther King, Jr. is shot |
| **1969** | Astronaut, Neil Armstrong is the first man to walk on the moon |
| **1970** | Nolan Bushnell invents the first video game, Pong |
| **1979** | Cellular phones invented |
| **1986** | The Chernobyl nuclear accident |
| **1989** | The fall of the Berlin Wall |
| **1993** | The Pentium Processor is invented |
| **2001** | Hijacked airplanes crash into the Twin Towers in New York City |

# TIMELINE IN HISTORY (CONT'D)

**2003**    Space Shuttle Columbia disintegrates on reentry
**2004**    An earthquake in the Indian Ocean triggers a Tsunami that causes casualties in a widespread area including Indonesia, Sri Lanka, India, and Thailand
**2005**    Julian Bond, Senator Tom Daschle, and Ginny Thornburgh are honorees of the Hurbert H. Humphrey Civil Rights Award sponsored by The Leadership Conference On Civil Rights

# CHAPTER NOTES

**Chapter One**
**The Calling**
1. Joan D. Hedrick, *Harriet Beecher Stowe: A Life* (New York: Oxford University Press, 1994), p. 207.

**Chapter Three**
**The Beecher Clan**
1. Joan D. Hedrick, *Harriet Beecher Stowe: A Life* (New York: Oxford University Press, 1994), p. 97.
2. Ibid., p. 239.
3. Ibid., p. 189.
4. Ibid., p. 190.

**Chapter Four**
**The Coming Transformation**
1. Joan D. Hedrick, *Harriet Beecher Stowe: A Life* (New York: Oxford University Press, 1994), p. 208.

2. Maureen E. Riedy, *Mothers in Uncle Tom's Cabin,* "Harriet Beecher Stowe," http://xroads.virginia.edu/~MA97/riedy/hbs.html
3. Stephen Railton, "Uncle Tom's Cabin and American Culture," http://jefferson.village.virginia.edu/utc/sitemap.html

**Chapter Five**
**The Writer and the War**
1. "Uncle Tom's Cabin," *Southern Literary Messenger,* December 1852, http://jefferson.village.virginia.edu/utc/reviews/rere24bt.html
2. Joan D. Hedrick, *Harriet Beecher Stowe: A Life* (New York: Oxford University Press, 1994), p. 258.
3. Ibid., p. 306.

# FURTHER READING

**For Young Adults**

Fradin, Dennis Brendell. *Bound for the North Star: True Stories of Fugitive Slaves.* Boston: Houghton Mifflin Co., 2000.

Macdonald, Fiona. *Women in 19th-Century America.* Lincolnwood, Illinois: Peter Bedrick Books, 2001.

Petry, Ann. *Harriet Tubman: Conductor of the Underground Railroad.* New York: HarperCollins, 1983.

Stowe, Harriet Beecher. *Uncle Tom's Cabin.* New York: Bantam Books, 1983.

Todras, Ellen H. *Angelina Grimke: Voice of Abolition.* North Haven, Connecticut: Linnet Books, 1999.

**Works Consulted**

Abbott, Lyman, D.D., and Rev. S. B. Halliday, eds. *Henry Ward Beecher: A Sketch of His Career.* (Quinnipiac University; Connecticut: American Publishing Company, 1887.)
Online at http://www.quinnipiac.edu/other/abl/etext/beecher/beechercomplete.html.

Collins, Gail. *America's Women: 400 Years of Dolls, Drudges, Helpmates, and Heroines.* New York: William Morrow, 2003.

Guynup, Sharon. "Cholera: Tracking the First Global Disease." *National Geographic News,* June 14, 2004.
Online at http://news.nationalgeographic.com/news/2004/06/0614_040614_tvcholera.html#main

Hedrick, Joan D. *Harriet Beecher Stowe: A Life.* New York: Oxford University Press, 1994.

Takach, James. "Frederick Stowe Could Not Escape the Lengthy Shadow of His Mother's Famous Novel, Uncle Tom's Cabin." *America's Civil War.* Volume 11, January 1999, p. 18.

PBS: *Africans in America,* Part IV: "The Underground Railroad."
http://www.pbs.org/wgbh/aia/part4/4p2944.html

**On the Internet**

C-SPAN: *American Writers,* "Harriet Beecher Stowe"
http://www.americanwriters.org/writers/stowe.asp

Harriet Beecher Stowe Center
http://www.harrietbeecherstowecenter.org/

National Geographic: *The Underground Railroad*
http://www.nationalgeographic.com/railroad/

# FURTHER READING (CONT'D)

PBS: *Africans in America,* 1998
> http://www.pbs.org/wgbh/aia/home.html
Railton, Stephen, and the University of Virginia. *Uncle Tom's Cabin & American Culture,* 2004
> http://jefferson.village.virginia.edu/utc/sitemap.html
Riedy, Maureen E. *Mothers in Uncle Tom's Cabin.* August 1997
> http://xroads.virginia.edu/~MA97/riedy/welcome.html

# GLOSSARY

**abolition**
(a-buh-LIH-shun)
the getting rid of a system or practice (especially slavery).

**controversial**
(con-truh-VER-shul)
marked by or capable of causing disagreement.

**dementia**
(dih-MENT-sha)
the loss of mental abilities.

**economy**
(eh-KAH-nuh-mee)
a system of production, distribution, and consumption, or the efficient use of resources.

**emancipate**
(ee-MAN-sih-payt)
to set free.

**ice floe**
(eys flo)
A large, flat mass of floating ice.

**gag rule**
(GAG-rul)
a law that prohibits discussion of a certain subject.

**literary**
(LIH-teh-rare-ee)
of or relating to literature or writing.

**momentum**
(mow-MEN-tum)
strength gained by motion or development.

**self-sufficient**
(self-suh-FIH-shunt)
able to provide for one's own needs without the help of others.

**suffragist**
(SUH-frah-jist)
someone who helps others, especially women, gain voting rights.

**temperance**
(TEM-prents)
the trait of avoiding excess; the act of avoiding alcoholic beverages.

# INDEX